Ideate Your Career: Why There Is No Such Thing As A Straight Career Path & What You Can Do About It

Eric S. Quon-Lee

DEDICATION

To all the ambitious and passionate dreamers and doers around the globe. Make your dreams and your visions come true. Don't let anything or anyone stop you from achieving them.

CONTENTS

ACKNOWLEDGMENTS

Many thanks to SZ and JH for their invaluable assistance in creating this e-book. Without their assistance, this e-book would be a lot less colorful and succinct.

Also, many thanks to my friends who spent countless hours debating with me about the right approaches to the issues addressed in this e-book. Without those insights, this e-book would be much poorer.

1 INTRODUCTION

This e-book has taken a curious path. It was born out of a personal observation that there is an increasing demand in the market after getting numerous requests for resume reviews and career advice.

A number of people have asked me who this e-book's audience is. It's for any individual who is looking to advance their career. I've gotten requests from individuals ranging from just out of college and post-MBA to mid career. In my opinion, that's okay as no one should be ashamed in asking for help. There are many legitimate reasons to ask for assistance, from being a complete newbie in all things career related to requiring a refresh in terms of up-to-date career advancement.

While it can be tempting to focus on the latest gimmicks when it comes to career advancement—we're looking at you, infographics—the concept is predominantly built on basic tenants that have been around forever. It isn't just a matter of what is old is new again. Understanding the true nature of career advancement means understanding both individual and group psychology and behavior.

Fundamentally, it's not only an understanding of yourself and your surroundings that will make you successful in your career—it's also the realization that everything you do is connected and part of a holistic ecosystem. To look specifically at what you need to do to ensure success, you need to focus on three specific components:

1) Capabilities
2) Networking
3) Experience

In the end, there are no clear or defined paths for an individual to follow. Every individual will take a different path regardless of how "standard" their education is. The reality is that the individual paths we follow are guided in many respects by the individualized experiences life will throw at us. How we respond and react to these experiences will be extremely critical in shaping our own individual career advancement.

Eric S. Quon-Lee
San Francisco, USA and Toronto, Canada

2 WHAT IS THE PURPOSE OF A CAREER?

For all the career advice out in the world, most of it only covers the basics. A truly promising employee may find it difficult to take things to the next level.

It isn't surprising that many career counsellors and advisors only focus on the basics. The reality is that there are more individuals in need of Career Advancement 101 than there are those who are willing to admit that they need help later on in their careers. But more advanced career guidance is a necessity due to the the fact that the very concept of "career" is shifting dramatically.

Both locally and globally, employees are increasingly feeling the pressure of an unstable business environment. From disappearing manufacturing jobs to growing youth unemployment, employment opportunities are far and few between.

It isn't that governments and individuals haven't tried to address lackluster employment growth. There has been growing investment in government job-retraining programs, and individuals are actively pursuing additional certifications to better their career chances.

Unfortunately, these efforts fail to take into account the changes that have occurred in the global economic landscape. The global economic foundation has been upended by a number of factors including:

1) **Automation:** Technology continues to replace the need for humans. The latest technology revolution led by artificial intelligence continues the trend.

2) **The Decline of Routine:** The nine-to-five routine has given way to "on-demand" work. This means that today's employees are on call 24/7 and don't have a set schedule as they run from one "on-demand" job to another to make end's meet.

3) **The Rise of Knowledge:** The decline of the manufacturing economy has lead to the rise of the knowledge economy. Increasingly, work is no longer reliant on mere brawn but the ability to outthink the competition with bits and bytes.

It's not just the global economic foundation that's changed but the path to prosperity as well.

A number of factors have fractured the prosperity path including:

1) **The Education Debt Burden:** While education is a crucial step to climb the economic ladder, the education debt is an increasingly risky burden. With wage stagnation and frequent employment changes, the ability of employees to carry education debt is increasingly limited. Indeed, as accreditation requirements continue to grow and employees are self-funding their skills upgrades, employees are finding their educational debt interfering with their personal growth.

2) **The Structured Ladder Deficit:** A clear career advancement path is no longer visible. In the Baby Boomer era, there was an unwritten contract that employees would stay with their employers in exchange for career growth opportunities. Today, that unwritten contract no longer exists.

The rise of the "on-demand" economy and the frenetic pace of change has broken the structured career ladder. For many, career advancement these days is less a straight linear growth ladder and more of a zig-zag fraught with increasing uncertainty and risk.

3) **The Entry-Level Job Dilemma:** In the past, freshly minted graduates could find employment that would "show them the ropes." Today, though, those entry level positions are increasingly disappearing thanks to a combination of technology and business complexity.

Technology has increasingly enabled organizations to automate a number of tasks that were in the past delegated to entry-level employees. From answering phones to collating documents, technology has increased employee self service for a number of basic tasks.

The benefits that technology has provided in terms of creating more openness and transparency cannot be understated. For example, the Internet has enabled individuals to access public records instantaneously and for free increasing accountability. However, with this openness and transparency comes the need for both businesses and employees to be mindful of intangible factors such as cultural differences and communication dissonance.

These factors increasingly require a heightened awareness of the overall business environment, which isn't necessarily provided solely through education but through experience. As such, companies are increasingly looking for more seasoned employees with both the education and the experience to effectively navigate this challenging business environment. This means it can be harder for more inexperienced candidates to break through.

4) **The Job Diversity and Mobility Problem:** Employees are being squeezed from both sides when it comes to the demands being placed on them. These pressures include:

   a) **Self Responsibility:** Employees are being squeezed by the challenging business environment, which not only demands that they lead and produce results, regardless of their level and responsibility, but also that they constantly upgrade their skills as new technologies emerge.

   b) **Technology Is Making Humans Obsolete:** Employees are being squeezed by technological advancements that are increasingly creeping up the employment food chain and making humans obsolete. With the rapid development of artificial intelligence and machine-to-machine learning, technology may soon replace humans at more challenging tasks such as driving.

How are these two pressures affecting job options and mobility for employees? Individuals who happen to be in dying professions and do not have the opportunities to adjust are increasingly finding their career paths constrained through no fault of their own.

In many respects, individuals who are in dying professions are in a death spiral. Trapped in shrinking industries and finding that their skills and experience have become obsolete, these workers haven't been given an alternative path to reposition their careers.

Make no mistake. The pace at which the global economy moves means no industry is safe. Indeed, Silicon Valley is not immune. The speed of this transition has caught many organizations and their employees off guard and scrambling to adapt to the new reality foisted upon them.

If the path is broken, what are we to do to fix it? There are no clear and easy solutions. There never were.

Indeed, the Band-Aid solutions that are being proffered merely move the chairs on a sinking *Titanic*. Today's supposed fixes don't address the fundamental changes that need to occur in the system to rebuild the broken career path, if there is a career path to rebuilt at all.

Like it or not, there weren't really defined career paths in the past, nor will there be in the future. The reality is that the "career path" we all yearn for is borne of individual need and psychology rather than reality.

While many would argue that there are defined paths, what they're really talking about are constructs in terms of the education and experience required to achieve the next level in one's career. How someone gets there is really up to them.

Many employees who believe that they will have a straight shot at career advancement don't understand that everything is customized. One's career is always about a zigzagging path rather than a straight line. Unfortunately, society gives false cues that a career is a straight line and fails to educate workers that those cues can be put together in a multitude of different ways.

One can argue that some of this is driven by the fact that we are inherently a social species that needs social interaction and companionship to thrive and survive. As such, we look for individuals with similar backgrounds and attitudes to whom we can relate and even emulate. This further drives the perception that there is a set career path to follow that enables individuals to "set and forget" their career aspirations, when in reality they need to constantly evolve and adapt their career aspirations.

Indeed, the changing business environment from both local and global perspectives has informed much of the writing in this e-book. Those looking for a simple step-by-step approach to career advancement are in for disappointment. The reality is that there is no one path for anyone to follow. It's true that we can use other successful individuals to act as potential guideposts, but in the end our individual circumstances will dictate what path our career advancement will take.

As such, this e-book is focused on how an individual can strengthen themselves in the changing business environment. Indeed, it is about becoming more self aware, self assured and independent as the global economy continues its dynamic charge forward. If the changes in today's global economy have taught us anything, it's that defining one's core values and beliefs rather than relying on a system or "path" is increasingly a necessity to not only survive but thrive.

This is why this e-book subscribes to five principles related to one's career advancement:

1) Know Who You Truly Are
2) Don't Be Afraid Of Who You Are
3) Real Leadership Comes From Self
4) Always Be Adapting (ABA)
5) Treat Yourself Like A Corporation

While the five principles may seem simple enough, they can be surprisingly difficult to implement. They not only require dedication and commitment, but also a true understanding of who one is beyond work. Individuals in today's marketplace can't let processes and systems define who they are.

This affects even those who say they knew from a young age that they were "destined" to accomplish their chosen career. We are a sum of our experiences and knowledge. The five principles are a reminder that we are constantly in flux and that we need to ground ourselves individually to not only understand ourselves better but to withstand the constant changes in today's global economy.

3 KNOW WHO YOU TRULY ARE

As we age, it's quite easy to understand why we constantly look to our past, particularly our childhood, and think that life was easier. Our childhoods are filled with rules and responsibilities, from how to cross the street to how to interact with other individuals. We were constantly being told what was socially acceptable (and what wasn't) by our parents, our teachers, and by public and private institutions and businesses.

While these rules and responsibilities are required to succeed in society, they leave little room for individuals to explore the fundamental core of who they are beyond widgets in the global economy. However, it isn't surprising that we as individuals don't take the time to explore who we are in this chaotic business environment. While the new global, technology-based economy has opened options for self learning, most of us are too busy to take advantage of it. It's a paradox that needs to be solved if we are to grow and advance as individuals and as a society.

The global economy and the technology that precipitated its rise has, in many respects, helped individuals expand their horizons in terms of personal growth opportunities. We can more easily acquire knowledge and find like-minded communities, and we can reach out to other groups from around the world to learn and grow in unprecedented ways. But for all the benefits that the global economy and associated technologies have brought, there are have been setbacks as well.

While the current marketplace has benefited a number of individuals with the rapid development on the knowledge economy, it has also left a significant number of workers by the wayside as the economy fundamentally shifts. Individuals who relied mainly on physical skill to achieve financial solvency are finding that they are either stuck in neutral or are gradually slipping into poverty. But even knowledge workers are starting to see drawbacks as well.

The constant change in today's global economy has made it difficult for even the most vaunted knowledge workers to keep pace without burning themselves out. Technologies, business models, and even markets are changing and reshaping at such a rapid pace that it's difficult for knowledge workers to keep on top of the changes, let alone ensure that their own skillsets are relevant. Indeed, it's not only skill-set relevance that knowledge workers must be concerned with in today's global economy, but also job relevance, as machine-to-machine learning and artificial intelligence is increasingly removing humans from the work equation. No wonder everyone from the manual laborer to the highly skilled knowledge worker is increasingly stressed.

So what are individuals supposed to do in this chaotic business environment? While many would suggest getting more certifications or doing more networking, the reality is that you'll first need to work on discovering the core of one's self.

Although you may be questioning the relevance of a very metaphysical and spiritual statement in a career advancement e-book, its relevance is increasingly important in this chaotic environment. The reality is those who don't value self-discovery in the same light as credentials, networking and sheer persistence, they're helping to perpetuate the next generation of "mid-life crisis professionals" who realize too little too late that they are stuck in situations that they didn't want.

For individuals to break out of the cycle of perpetual career misery, the dynamism of the global economy is forcing them to truly discover what they want from life itself, not just from their careers. In other words, you need to:

1) **Find Your Passion:** In Silicon Valley, every founder needs to be "passionate and committed," because there will be an inevitable number of ups and downs as their start-up grows. Without that passion and commitment, it's easy to make a mistake by taking what appears to be the easy way out, when in fact it's really just undoing all the progress a start-up has made.

The same goes for an individual looking for career advancement.

Choosing a profession that is "hot" today doesn't necessarily guarantee long-term career success. Indeed, if today's knowledge-based economy has proven anything, it's that choosing a career solely on money or short-term prospects is setting one's self up for constant frustration. You may feel like you're running from one hamster wheel to another without making any real progress.

2) **Discover What You Truly Want to Do Devoid of Social and Career Trappings:** It's very easy to slip into the warm embrace of social and career trappings. Whether it's a title that implies power and influence or the perks and benefits that come with specific roles and levels, the reality is that these things don't make the individual—they're merely theatre dressing with little substance.

Social and career trappings are much like the "keeping up with the Joneses" materialism that has caused so many individuals to go into perpetual debt. Instead of discovering what they truly value from a non-materialistic perspective, these people replace values with constant one-upmanship that merely leads to more debt and misery.

Smart individuals realize that in today's unpredictable business environment, the perks and privileges that come with certain roles are fleeting and illusory. Indeed, they don't call social and career trappings "golden handcuffs" for nothing. They bind individuals to roles and career paths that may not necessarily be right for them, because there's no separation between personal and career goals.

It can be difficult to separate personal and social goals from career ones. We are social creatures, and we prefer the company of our fellow human beings to being alone. It is what creates community bonds and what makes it so difficult for individuals to discover what they truly want out of their career. It can be done, however.

It's important to think about both the present and past to help clarify what you truly want in a career. Like it or not, we can't run from our past no matter how many credentials or certifications we have. That doesn't mean we can't shape our careers. Indeed, we can use the past to help shape the present and the future.

The cumulative hopes, dreams, and experiences of our past helps us determine what we truly want to do in our careers (and in our lives in general). These experiences have taught us what we like, what we don't like, and what drives us forward. They help us shape a story of what we're truly passionate about and what we want out of our career.

3) **Ensure There's a Separation Between Career and Personal:** One of the biggest issues with today's global economy, particularly in Silicon Valley, is that work and personal seem inextricably intertwined with each other. It's easy to confuse finding passion in your career with being passionate about life. Career passion is a necessary driver to enable individuals to power through the inevitable bureaucracy and needless delays that careers bring. It's critical to have that passion as it allows you to find the mental energy to not only push forward but the creativity to find solutions to roadblocks.

Separating career and life passion can be tricky when you hear of successful entrepreneurs who have managed to build businesses from their hobbies. While such success stories are to be admired, the reality is that it isn't the full story. Yes, these hobbyists-turned-entrepreneurs have managed to turn a personal passion into a business, but it's easy to forget that it's likely only one passion amongst many.

These entrepreneurs probably have many other personal passions that they will never turn into businesses. They understand that keeping a part of their lives separate from their careers is critical to their professional and personal success.

The ability to truly recharge—without having to worry about deadlines, deliverables, or career repercussions—is not only liberating to the psyche, but also necessary for you to achieve the best you can in your career. Today's knowledge economy is increasingly more about creative thought leadership than production. To achieve the utmost productivity, you need to find outlets where you can disengage your brain from career-oriented tasks.

4) **Believe in Yourself:** Ultimately, you have to find a way to believe in yourself regardless of the circumstances you find yourself in. Physical success can only temporarily provide comfort to someone that's unsure of themselves.

Indeed, finding personal fulfillment is critical for external success, whether physical or otherwise. Through our subtle and direct actions, we exude how confident or how self-assured we are. These cues will determine how we are treated and how we will succeed. No amount of material wealth can compensate for that.

Ultimately, finding one's self is half the battle. It's an extremely difficult task, but it's crucial to learning how to express one's personal values. Although it's particularly difficult in our highly dynamic times, it's essential for achieving rapid career advancement.

4 DON'T BE AFRAID OF WHO YOU ARE

Making the most of personal expression is one of the biggest challenges facing employees in today's business environment. It goes beyond the age-old battles of political and religious expression, and in fact stems from the deeply rooted values that define one's self. Indeed, personal expression sets the tone for one's interactions with both professional colleagues and people in their personal life.

We're all familiar with well-worn Hollywood stereotypes about various careers, whether it's the sleazy used car salesperson or the friendly neighborhood doctor. Of course, the reality is much more complex.

The truth is, we're trained from a young age to believe in these kinds of Hollywood stereotypes because of the fact that, for the most part, we're trained to be widgets. As individuals, we need some type of structure or framework to make sense of society, and we use education to ensure that the "basics" of structure are indoctrinated. That indoctrination continues throughout one's educational path and into the workforce as well.

The modern agricultural and industrial movements required individuals to conform in a systematic way, become "cogs in the machine" if you will, which can be easily replaced. The upside is that it lead to an overall higher standard of living and productivity around the world. However, that system of conformity is under attack not from its failure but from its own success.

Thanks to increased productivity and scientific advancements that have resulted from the success of these movements, we are slowly moving towards a new phase in employment, a knowledge-based one. While many believe that the knowledge-based economy is merely another "transition," it's a dramatically different transition thanks to automation. It is a transition to an age where the individual is valued more than the system.

Thanks to the technological improvements that have occurred, we are increasingly able to transition away from using humans as mere "cogs in the machine," relying instead on machines for repetitive and boring tasks. This has meant that individualism is increasingly more valued than merely acting as a "cog in the machine." That being said, individualism didn't suddenly spring forth from the new knowledge economy. It has always been valued but in a more limited scope.

Every industry values creativity and individualism, but the degree to which those traits are valued varies. People sometimes forget that even in the agricultural and industrial eras, individualism was highly prized and valued. We just named it a different way. Instead of individualism, we called it the "C-suite" or, more recently, "entrepreneurialism." As a society, we venerate successful entrepreneurs or Hollywood celebrities who have made their individuality a trademark of their success.

Unfortunately, instead of training for individuality, we train for conformity. Individuals are trained to follow the system with the belief that they will be rewarded through promotions and raises. But in reality, to be a successful entrepreneur or make it to the C-suite, you've got to be noticed and that means shining a light on your individuality. Like it or not, merely doing your assigned tasks well is not the way to climb the ranks. Only by standing out in the crowd can you succeed, and the best way to do that is by demonstrating your individuality.

We all bring our individual values to our careers. Whether you're a manual laborer or a knowledge professional, it's your individuality that brings quality and conscientiousness to the job—not the roles and responsibilities defined for the position.

From the manual labor perspective, accomplished workers bring their own creativity and individuality to the assembly line, from developing their own way of accomplishing their set task to showing diligence in the quality of the work they complete. And, in fact, the care taken in assembly will be reflected in the final product.

While you might think it would be easier to see how creativity and individualism are beneficial in the knowledge economy, the reality is their value can be harder to perceive. It's much easier for someone in a high-profile role to demonstrate their individuality than it is for a junior or mid-level employee.

We're still in the midst of a transition to a full knowledge economy, which means many workers are still expected to complete repetitive and sometimes unchallenging tasks. Automation is slowly taking over the completion of repetitive tasks, but the reality is that there are still roles in the knowledge economy that require a human presence.

Fundamentally, however, it has been difficult for employees to express their individuality in the workplace. We are constantly encouraged to conform through social, organizational or peer pressure. Smart individuals know how to conform yet at the same time express their individuality, a hard balance that's worth continuously trying to master.

In investment banking, analysts are expected (and taught) to conform to the industry's standards. This means the same style of suits, the same luggage, the same speech cadence, etc. If an analyst is able to climb up the ladder to vice president, then he or she's allowed a little bit of personal flair. This could be through multi-colored socks or a pocket square. If that person reaches the highest rung on the ladder, he or she can go all out in terms of showing personality, whether through hobbies or personal trophies at work.

In today's new industries, however, employees need to express their individuality, creativity, and passion immediately. Unfortunately, for a significant number of people, expressing those traits doesn't come naturally, because years of educational and societal conformity have created in them a significant amount of self-doubt and confusion. If creativity and individuality are to be the norm, how does one find ways to demonstrate those traits while still being gainfully employed?

There is no one path for individuals to take as they discover how to express their individuality and creativity. Each industry, position, and culture will have different paths to enable that creativity to be expressed. That being said, there are some foundational elements that are essential including:

1) **Know Yourself, but Recognize That You Are a Growing and Dynamic Individual:** There's a reason that "Know Yourself" is before "Don't Be Afraid to Express Yourself." Truly understanding yourself means that you aren't afraid of change and you aren't afraid of expressing yourself. You aren't beholden to the whims of your

position or career, but you truly understand who you are regardless of your circumstances.

That being said, who you are isn't static. Whether we recognize it or not, we are constantly growing because we are constantly learning. That learning occurs because we wake up in the morning and experience new wonders regardless of how small they may seem.

2) **Don't Only Be Self Aware, Be Externally Aware as Well:** Growth happens more easily if one is self-aware. What does that mean? It means that we recognize that we are constantly learning and growing, and the best way to do that is to be aware of those changes. It means that you need to take the time to understand how those learnings are influencing your perception of the world around you. However, self-awareness is only one part of the equation—you need to be aware of the external as well.

Context is everything, and it must be respected even when you are being yourself. Just as there needs to be respect for who you are as an individual, there must be respect for the context and the situation that you are in.

3) **Be Ready to Answer Why You Are Who You Are:** People are curious. It's one of humanity's greatest gifts, but for many it can be hard to deal with. Most people don't expect to be questioned about what they do or why they do things. The reality is the exact opposite. As such, it is up to us to better understand why we do things. Simply saying that things have always been done this way won't cut it. We need to be honest with ourselves about why we do things to provide a concrete justification for our actions.

This awareness is a continuation of self-discovery. We are the culmination of our past experiences, and understanding how our past experiences have influenced us is not only critical to our self-awareness but also to helping others understand why we do things the way we do.

4) **Understand the System and the Processes Around You:** In the end, you are representing the brand and the organization that you are working for, and that means that your behavior on the job is a reflection of the organization. It also provides context in terms of where your individuality can truly shine and where it cannot.

This is why it's critical that one understands the difference between self and the job. Without that separation, the individual will not be happy, because the job cannot truly represent them and never will. We must realize that a job is a means to an end but is not a means to living. As such, it's critical to understand the system and processes that surround you.

Why? Because the way we express our individuality is constrained by those processes and systems. The job isn't supposed to conform to all our desires and preferences, but it is supposed to provide us the means to fund our creative and individual endeavors. That being said, it doesn't mean that the system and processes can't integrate our individuality and creativity, even if just in small ways.

5) **Be Open-Minded:** If you are truly comfortable with yourself, you'll be willing to learn new things and be open to new processes. What constitutes self isn't the clothes we wear or the position we hold; it's whether or not we can justify to our own soul why we do things and if it is right for us. But doing that requires flexibility. We need to be open minded to explore different way to doing things and determine whether they are appropriate for us as individuals.

6) **Remember That You Can Change the Perception of You to Be What You Want:** As the old saying goes, perception is reality. Whether we like it or not, how society views us as individuals is driven by biases, stereotypes, and interactions based on an agreed-upon framework. If the perception of us feels in sync with our personal values, then there is alignment. If it does not, we must decide whether or not to change our behavior.

Giving up one's core values should never be in the equation, however. Rather we need to try to understand why people perceive us the way they do and then decide whether it's something we're comfortable with or it's something we have to work on.

Take, for example, an individual that might believe they're highly decisive, but the perception from others is that they're not. That person might believe that because they make decisions quickly and decisively in their personal life, it's automatically true of their professional lives as well. The reality can be the exact opposite, however, because that person may be making decisions based on their own biases and timelines and not ones in a professional environment involving other people.

Such situations can create significant individual bias and distort one's perception, particularly if it's challenged. As such, it can be extremely difficult to separate one's own beliefs from reality. It is critical that we have the self awareness to acknowledge that our perception might be flawed. It's equally critical that if we truly cherish a value as part of our core, we take action to ensure that the rest of the world sees us for what we want to be.

5 REAL LEADERSHIP COMES FROM SELF

Many people have the false perception that leadership is thrust upon people in a clear and coherent manner. The reality is that it subtly sneaks up on people with little or no warning. Leadership is earned not only through the ability of individuals to continue to do their individually assigned tasks while at the same time being able to manage and delegate new responsibilities to others. Ultimately, leadership is one of the hardest things to master.

Leadership is an important skill set for everyone to learn from the C-suite down to the entry-level employee. But it's also undergoing a transformation as well. Workers are no longer being seen as mere physical inputs into a system that produces other physical inputs but rather as engines whose creativity and adaptability reign supreme.

What this means is that the old "command and control" style of management is increasingly being replaced with a more collaborative and team-oriented approach to management that emphasizes the growth and development of the individual. Indeed, while some are still fans of the "Darth Vader" approach to management—which treats workers as expendable peons who exist only to fulfill strict production quotas—the reality is that type of management style is being replaced out of practical necessity.

As automation makes a quota-driven system increasingly irrelevant, workers are less frequently used to man the production system but rather to prime it through creative design and innovation.

As such, the nature of management has changed. It's no longer primarily about efficiently managing to tight schedules, although that does still play a role. Instead, the primary focus of management is now developing the techniques and skills to motivate and coach fellow workers to new heights, not only in their careers but in their personal lives as well.

To be a great leader, one has to understand themselves first, and that's a never-ending quest. The longer we live and the more experiences we accumulate, the more we change. Our thoughts change, our beliefs change, and our understanding of the world around us changes. All for the better.

As we change, we have an opportunity to impart to others the learnings that we have accumulated through our experiences. Fundamentally, that's what true leadership is. We have a duty as leaders to go beyond merely feeding the massive machine by empowering individuals to find themselves while navigating the turbulent waters of the global economy.

6 SELF-LEADERSHIP

As mentioned throughout this e-book, leadership and career advancement don't spring from a learning process or by adhering to a framework. Rather, true leadership is driven by an understanding of one's self.

Some might argue that leadership is driven by the position an individual occupies. While that may have been the "old way" of leadership, it's problematic in the following ways:

1) **Motivation Deficit:** Merely "working a job," versus treating the job with the same care as you would family, yields completely different results not only in terms of end product quality but in terms of business growth. It's all too easy to treat individuals as widgets, particularly with automation rapidly encroaching on jobs across industries. But the reality is that as workers continue to provide the bulk of the labor, it's critical that they feel motivated to complete their jobs in as effective and high-quality manner as possible.

2) **Burnout Through Endless Churn:** Employees at all levels desire advancement both personally and professionally. That advancement can come in different forms, whether it's completing a project or learning a new skill. Employees get frustrated when they have to constantly redo tasks because of needless strategic or operational churn. Whether it's never-ending "zombie" tasks or projects that are endlessly reworked, these are the kinds of situation that will send employees looking for alternatives outside of their existing employment.

3) **A Lack of Foresight & Innovation:** The constant pressure that's placed upon individuals by the churn of old leadership limits the ability of an organization to react to and think about changes in the business environment. As the organization and individuals within the organization scramble to fulfill the whims and desires of poor leadership, they don't have the time, energy or foresight to realize that the business environment around them has changed. Which of course, leaves them unable to react to that change.

If the "old way" of leadership isn't going to work, then what is? In many respects, it's a change of what we define as leadership. Instead of looking externally for leadership, organizations are increasingly looking for "self-leadership." What is "self-leadership"?

In many respects, self-leadership is not only about "self-awareness" but also about "self-actualization." First, though, we need to get some clarity on the meaning of "self-awareness."

7 SELF-AWARENESS

Self-awareness is a concept that's been bantered about for decades and grows increasingly relevant as we continue to transition to the knowledge economy. For many, it is still a term associated with "free spirits" or "hippies" and not one that's seen as relevant to career strategy. In reality, self-awareness is essential to charting your own career path.

In many respects, self-awareness is probably the best defense in these turbulent career times. Whether we acknowledge it or not, we have been trained both consciously and subconsciously to identify with our careers. One doesn't have to think hard about how intertwined we are with our careers. Within the first 30 seconds of an introduction, whether at the office or at a dinner party, the question that's inevitably asked is: "What do you do?"

It's not surprising this is one of the first questions out of people's mouths. With a significant majority of our lives devoted to the workplace, it's easy to see how it becomes the be-all and end-all of our existence. Indeed, in many respects, it has also gotten worse over time as start-up culture and the on-demand economy continues to blur divisions that exist between work and life. The problem is that while on the one hand start-up culture and the on-demand economy has dissolved the work-life balance, it's also made less likely for individuals to express their identity primarily through their work.

In the past, one's career was not only easily identified but also consistent. Individuals didn't make significant changes in their career. If you had friends you hadn't seen in ages, there was a high probability that if you encountered them, they would be at the same firm, in the same industry but with a more senior position. Today, however, that predictability no longer exists.

It's not only the dizzying speed of technological change that is uprooting career norms: the pace at which it's impacting the business environment is also disconcerting to individuals. We have seen how rapidly old "titans of industry" can rapidly fall and be replaced with new industry leaders who only a few years ago were considered "start-ups." The fast pace at which these changes occur makes it difficult for any individual to state that they have a set career or work in an established industry, thus leaving many individuals feeling rudderless and devoid of purpose. This is where the need for individual "self-awareness" is critical.

But what is "self-awareness"? It's a combination of a number of elements that ultimately determine who someone truly is. These "self-awareness" elements include:

1) **An Understanding of Self Value:** While we are all taught at a young age the various cultural and social norms and values that are inherent in our respective societies, many of us forget that we have free will to determine how we will individually interpret those signals. It's remarkably easy for individuals to forget that we have this free will as we literally are transitioned from one structured system to another (e.g., school to work) where we're conditioned to respect and follow a set of rules.

Indeed, for all the education that's provided to individuals concerning values and structure, there's no acknowledgement that it's up to every individual how they interpret those values. It's this individual interpretation of overall values that allows for a diversity of opinion in society. What does this have to do with an individual's self-value?

There is a difference between agreeing in general terms to a common value and integrating it into your daily life. For example, many people state that they believe in helping others, but for some that may mean a financial contribution while for others it means direct action. Neither approach is wrong, but those critical differences in interpretation define an individual's values.

Why is it so important to have a deep and detailed understanding of one's individual values? An awareness of how you practice your core values is critical to formulating the foundation for a truly satisfying career path.

As individuals and as a society, we're far too reliant on generalizations to provide an understanding of what we as individuals personally represent. When someone tells us they're in business development, we may jump to false preconceptions about their personality or values. A common stereotype about business-development individuals is that they are personable and extroverted, when they could in fact be the polar opposite, while at the same time still being good at their role.

A stereotype about a profession shouldn't be viewed as a good representation of the values that an individual holds dear. Indeed, it can be the complete opposite, and thus it's critical that individuals know what values are truly important to them.

Indeed, organizations are starting to understand that cultural values are a critical aspect to growing and sustaining a high-performing organization. Culture as defined by common shared values is critical to enabling the organization to survive difficult times as well as to grow in a sustainable fashion. As such, organizations are increasingly looking at the cultural fit of new employees as a critical factor (in addition to skills) when hiring.

What does that mean for individuals? It's crucial that they have difficult conversations with themselves about their own values, regardless of the stereotypes and preconceptions that they have been taught over their lives. Without this deep understanding of one's values, there can be no growth and there can be no career, at least according to the new definition of career.

In today's career paths, over-valuing marketing slogans or interpretations of organizational culture is the new equivalent of running after titles or money. The sad reality is that many individuals have transitioned from running on one hamster wheel (e.g., the pursuit of wealth and power) to another (e.g., the pursuit of hipness). Without identifying what you truly value individually, you'll likely find yourself constantly adrift and moving from one organization to another wondering why you don't fit in.

2) **An Understanding of Self Skill:** Another misinterpretation that we

have all bought into is confusing accreditation and certification with individual skills. Accreditation and credentials are important signals in our current social and business environment, but they do not necessarily represent individual skills, which are more important than ever.

In an age where individualism is moving to the forefront of society and business, it's increasingly necessary for people to truly discover what skills they possess. Indeed, while accreditation and certification provide some advantages in terms of signaling, organizations and individuals are discovering they must conduct their own due diligence to look for the specific skills they need to fulfill open roles.

Why are individual skills increasingly more important? It goes well beyond the rise of individualism and gets to the heart of the changes that are bubbling up in society in general. Similar to what is happening with manual tasks, "common" skills are increasingly in abundance in the general workforce. There is an expectation that potential employees are equipped with the "common" skills required to survive the workforce such as typing and communicating. Organizations are increasingly not only looking for the next level of individual skills but they are also looking for the "complete package".

What are the next level of individual skills required? While you might think they'd be technical skills such as those frequently found in STEM professions, the reality is far different. The skills that are increasingly demanded and sought after are (a) emotional intelligence skills and (b) communications skills. Why are these two types of skills so important?

Increasingly, with repetitive tasks being automated and tools more available to anyone, having the right skills to communicate effectively to a wide variety of audiences is a necessity. Indeed, being able to convince sufficient numbers of individuals to buy into an idea is THE difference between success and failure. While technology and new business models have made it possible for "niche" ideas to thrive and survive, legacy business models are still at the fore, and this means that "size matters."

If it isn't only accreditation and credentials that are driving individual careers forward but the holistic application of individual skills, what is an individual to do to identify and learn these critical skills required in the new business environment?

Fundamentally, all of this requires a willingness to attempt to be "self-aware." For many, though, the question is how? There are no simple and clear cut answers, but there are some fundamental things that can be done to gain self-awareness:

a) **Ask a Diversity of Trusted Advisors:** How one is interpreted is always in the eye of the beholder. For all the efforts that people or even organizations undertakes to manage their brand and image, they cannot enforce their singular brand. The reality is that every individual will have their own brand interpretation due to free will and freedom of thought.

   While it may be impossible to enforce a singular brand image, it is possible to manage it, so that it is a true reflection of your individual values. Indeed, for individuals to succeed, it's critical to carefully manage their image while remaining true to their core values.

   To do so, it's vital to ask a diversity of trusted advisors around you. In many respects, this is the start of opening yourself up to becoming self-aware in a relatively safe environment. These should be individuals who you trust and whose opinions you value.

   One critical thing of note, however, is that you should seek a "diversity" of opinions. It's too easy to form an "echo chamber" when it comes to asking trusted advisors for their opinion. The only way you can truly understand how your brand is perceived by society is to make sure your "advisory panel" reflects society's heterogenous mix.

b) **Be Willing to Listen:** One of the hardest tasks that a self-aware individual usually has to learn is the willingness to listen to feedback. It can be difficult to believe what we're being told, particularly when the feedback doesn't fit our positive self-perception. It can feel like a crushing blow to the ego. That being said, however, it is how we respond to tough feedback that differentiates someone as being truly self-aware.

   Self-awareness means acknowledging the pain of having your ego bruised and then reflecting on the feedback's validity toward achieving your long-term objectives.

c) **Be Willing to Ask the Hard Questions:** It's only natural for us to want to stay within our safe bubbles, and the easiest way to do that is to fail to ask the hard questions. These are the kinds of questions that can rock you fundamentally if you're not sure of your core values. But they are also crucial to face if you want to continue to push toward self-fulfillment and self-awareness.

8 SELF-ACTUALIZATION

While self-awareness is crucial to succeed today's society, self-actualization is a vital next step. It's the difference between merely understanding yourself and using that understanding to make your values come alive.

It's easy in today's chaotic business environment to blame others for a failure to achieve one's goals. Whether it's bureaucracy or a supposed lack of opportunity, there are an infinite number of justifications one can give for a failure to achieve goals. It cannot be understated that the system does indeed throw up roadblocks against everyone to achieve their goals. It is the nature of the beast. Whether it's achieving the dream of being a singer or being the first in a family to achieve a post-secondary degree, the obstacles that one must overcome can be daunting.

The reality, though, is that these turbulent times provide opportunity to those who want to achieve their dreams if they are willing to go beyond the traditional norms of what defines success and how to achieve it.

The unprecedented disruption that we are seeing due to new technologies and business models has provided individuals with the opportunity to achieve their dreams if they are willing to see the possibilities and expand beyond the normal definitions of success. Indeed, for too long, individuals have been taught that both consciously and subconsciously that there is only one true path to success.

From entrepreneurs to CEOs, we constantly believe that those who have succeeded have taken a well-trodden path that we can all follow. But the reality is the paths that these trailblazers have taken are unique just like themselves. While certain behaviors can and should be replicated (e.g., persistence), everyone must find their own individual to achieve their goals. That is the overall theme of this e-book.

Indeed, the biggest takeaway that individuals can take away from entrepreneurs and CEOs besides their successful behaviors is their ability to project their beliefs, values, and individualism in a convincing manner to the world. There are many of us that mistake "machismo" and brute force with the ability to convince individuals of a viewpoint.

Unfortunately, "machismo" and brute force don't work in the long-term, in any context. The reality is that individuals who are only convinced through intimidation will eventually find way to avoid or minimize their participation in ideals or directions that they don't believe in. This is particularly troublesome in today's business environment, where gaining complete buy-in from individuals is crucial to get the best performance out of them.

So how is this relevant to self-actualization and self-leadership? While today's technology has enabled individuals to turn their dreams into reality, you must still convince large groups of people of the importance of those dreams. In many respects, it means overcoming the old adage that if you build the best technology, it will get adopted. The sad reality is that without the ability to convince others that your technology is the best one to adopt, another average technology will be the standard. We've seen that time and time again throughout the ages.

If self-actualization is about more than just about doing something then what are its other components? There are two key additional elements required:

1) Self-Management
2) External Management

Self-Management

As constantly iterated throughout this e-book, true career growth requires unlearning what we've been taught throughout our childhood and careers. For too long, we've been trained how to be widgets within the larger system. The reality of today's business environment is that we need to be less widget-like and more independent, hence the increasing need for self-management.

What is self-management? To begin with, it requires the realization that you are in control of your destiny. Yes, there will always be obstacles, whether social or systemic, but the reality is that it's ultimately up to us as individuals to drive forward.

Once you've made peace with this concept, there are four key principles to self-management:

1) **You Are in the Driver's Seat & It Can Be Lonely to Drive:** The shocking reality that we seem to have forgotten is that you and you alone are in the driver's seat of your own destiny. We spend so much time and resources training individuals to work in groups and as part of a team but not enough on their own forward momentum.

   One of the toughest realizations for high performers is that the higher they climb, the lonelier it can be. This is because, as you climb the ladder, you'll have less access to a support network as you deal with the overwhelming pressures of responsibility for individuals working with you as well as the entire organization. Some leaders learn to cope and find healthy outlets to ensure they don't crack under the pressure. Others unfortunately crack under the pressure and end up not only hurting themselves but the organizations and the individuals that have placed their faith in them.

2) **Finding a Balance Between Instinctual Action & Thinking It Through:** For all the societal refinement and training that we undergo, our raw, natural instincts also play a huge role in our responses. Whether it's an individual's quickness to anger if they feel they've been personally slighted or our emotional reaction to a powerfully crafted and presented speech, our natural instincts continue to affect us.

   On the other hand, society teaches us behaviors and actions that may make us feel unnatural and robotic. In many respects, these behaviors have enabled us to fit into a highly structured business environment.

   In today's changing business environment, a balance between the robotic and the instinctual is more important than ever. The jobs that once taught us to be robotic are now being fulfilled by actual robots. Therefore it's important that individuals find what makes them unique, as creativity and innovation are the name of the game. However, there is still a need to find a balance between individual brilliance and the ability to work in a team.

We all know the stereotype of the genius who is incredibly brilliant but impossible to work with. While that brilliance may allow them to climb to certain heights, the reality is that their inability to temper their neuroses diminishes their powers of persuasion. That's particularly limiting in today's society, as the fluidity of change is enabling individuals to have a greater impact than ever before.

3) **Don't Be Afraid of Being Wrong as Long as You Did Everything Possible & Are Willing to Learn:** "You only have one shot." "This is your only chance, don't blow it." Everyone has heard this and similar phrases throughout their career. While such statements are valid—first impressions usually are hard to overcome—they reinforce for many a natural fear of making a mistake when they should be taking every experience as a learning opportunity.

Whether we acknowledge it or not, successful individuals have made their fair share of mistakes before achieving great accomplishments. The difference is that they learn from their mistakes, and remember them the next time to ensure that they don't make the same error twice.

As long as you have done your absolute best in terms of preparation, it's okay to be wrong or to make a mistake. Of course, that requires your full honesty about whether you have done the due diligence and preparation beforehand, or if you just did something sloppily at the last minute. In other words, an individual needs to find the balance between being overly self-critical and acknowledging one's weaknesses to improve going forward.

The ability to learn from your mistakes is one of the hardest skills to learn. It can be ego-crushing, as it means acknowledging that we don't know everything, and it also requires coming to terms with the fact that we are all constantly learning no matter the age.

4) **It's Not Just About the Work:** The new post-modern business

work environment has moved from striving for work-life balance to Silicon Valley–style work 24/7. Too many of us are unable to turn our brain off after work even when surrounded by close friends and family.

As employees climb the ranks in an organization, the pressure and responsibility they face grows along with demands on their personal time and resources. They must contend with a never-ending stream of demands and decisions that impact not only the health of the organization but the lives of numerous individuals. Stressful times indeed.

The reality of human nature dictates that even an individual with the greatest alignment in work-life balance needs to step away from it completely. Indeed, high-performing individuals have a tendency to forget that breaking their routine and disconnecting from their job's constant buzz of is critical to ensure quality work going forward. Although many of us like to think we're machines capable of working 24/7, we all need complete breaks from our routine if we are to be as creative and innovative as possible. Smart organizations acknowledge this.

External Management

As with everything in life, there is a dualistic nature that needs to be understood when it comes to self-actualization. It's not only self-management that an individual needs to develop but external management as well.

The reality of today's globalized and highly integrated business environment means that it's critical for an individual to manage their external perception to ensure that their vision and ideals are adopted by as many individuals as possible. But what is meant by external management? In many respects, it boils down to three characteristics:

1) **Think of Leadership as Acting:** As has been constantly iterated in this e-book, one needs to have a core understanding of their values to succeed in this dynamic business environment. It enables you to exude an aura of confidence and knowledge that's critical to convincing other people to buy into your vision. However, understanding one's core values and exuding confidence are only part of the game. The other part is acting the role that individuals

want you to play.

Successful individuals know how to use psychology to get people to support their dreams. We've all seen it. Whether it's a successful politician who has inspired crowds through electrifying speeches or an actor who seems to nail every role they get, successful individuals know how to mesmerize a crowd into submission.

It's crucial to figure out how to tell a truly convincing story to get others on board with your plans. The best way to do this is to understand how to combine your ideas with a powerful presentation style. In other words, how to act.

Actors must merge their knowledge with their ability to convince someone of that knowledge in an emotional and compelling fashion. While content matters, how that content is conveyed is equally, if not more, important. It's how we as a species have learned to communicate and understand each other.

Acting is about getting the audience to buy in both consciously and subconsciously to a message. Presenting one's dream and vision is no different.

2) **You Are Allowed to Have an Opinion, Just Be Prepared to Defend It:** Many of us been taught or believe that our opinions don't matter. This may come from having been told to keep quiet rather than expressing oneself, or from feeling like your opinion will be ignored.

However, healthy debate and discussion are crucial in today's dynamic global economy. It's critical to making sure that an organization doesn't make decisions based on groupthink and has fully considered all the options that are available. Debate should be considered a healthy part of the decision-making process.

What scares most people about debate is that they believe (a) they'll be disrespectful toward authority or (b) they'll be disrespectful toward others. Both concerns are valid: it's important to approach debate in a respectful manner. Indeed, getting comfortable with respectful debate is another critical lesson that we need to learn to grow in today's dynamic economy.

So how does one engage in respectful debate? Here are some key principles:

a) **Focus on the Facts:** It's amazing how, during debates, we can slip into emotional arguments rather than fact-based ones. Relying on this style of debate means you need less preparation and also enables you to make disingenuous arguments that may work to your political advantage.

In today's dynamic business environment, however, a debate that's less focused on facts and more on emotions is a recipe for disaster. With the growth of artificial intelligence and the increased complexity and accessibility of Big Data, there are fewer excuses for not making analytical-based decisions. Indeed, if organizations want to ensure they remain competitive, they must find ways of training their organizations as well as their individuals to make decisions based on a combination of human instinct and data.

b) **Don't Focus on the Deliverer:** Too many of us have learned poor debate behaviors via television and politicians. These ineffective debaters rely on their own biases and stereotypes about their opponents rather than focusing on the facts.

Sometimes, it's easier to blame the deliverer of a difficult message than to acknowledge that their viewpoint might be the right one, even if it goes against our own beliefs.

c) **You Are Allowed to Take Control. Just Remember to REALLY Listen:** It can be tough to learn to take control of a work situation. Because we are constantly taught to defer to authority, it can be difficult to challenge someone even when we have the knowledge and platform to do so.

In addition, taking control inherently forces us to exit our comfort zone and grow by taking on additional responsibility. As much as we like to believe that leadership is taught in seminars and in educational institutions, most leaders will tell you that true leadership is taught on the battlefield of experience.

It's vital to learn how to take control in a respectful manner, particularly as the top-down management style continues to decline. Treating individuals on a project or in an organization as widgets provides comfort to leaders who are used to managing tasks in a mechanical manner. Unfortunately, though, it's not an effective way to motivate employees to leverage their maximum creativity and innovation.

Today's talent pool is looking for organizations that not only respect their values but also their creativity and innovation. They believe that top-down command and control management is antithetical to not their efforts and their ability to produce the best work possible. By not taking the opportunity to lead by listening and collaboration, leaders miss out on the opportunity to gain as much as possible from these employees.

What creative and innovative individuals are looking for are leaders who can communicate and execute their vision by convincing team members to join the journey through deliberate discussion (rather than brute force). In other words, individuals want leaders who listen and who treat their team members as important contributors.

Leaders of course must find a way to balance the competing demands between listening and getting the concrete results required of them. As always there is a fine line between deliberate discussion and being a pushover, as well as between leading and being arrogant. Leadership is very much about finding a balance between two seemingly opposed extremes. Finding the right mix is the key to effective management.

9 ALWAYS BE ADAPTING (ABA)

Today's career environment has never been more unstable. Multiple factors are changing in the business landscape, including accepted management norms (less command and control and more team-oriented approaches); career tenure (less single organization and more multiple organizations); and even the very nature of work (less nine-to-five routine and more gig economy). This increasing instability has caused significant stress on the workforce, because the norms that have been taught are increasingly less applicable.

Indeed, the old adages from traditional career counseling increasingly seem antiquated. Some examples that have definitely not stood the test of time:

1) **Climbing the Ladder at One Organization:** In the past it may have been more profitable to stay at one organization and climb the ladder, but that's increasingly a fool's game in today's complex, globalized economy. Unless you're a consistent star performer who accelerates through the ranks rapidly, the reality of the situation is that staying at one organization is not only financially disastrous but potentially even career-ending.

2) **Settling for Repetition:** While it's true that there's some amount of repetition required to learn a new skill, there are both individual and career limits to this. Because repetitive tasks and activities are being handled through automation, the need for employees to complete those tasks is shrinking over time.

3) **Believing a Post-Secondary Degree Is the Only Educational Accreditation Required to Advance:** A post-secondary degree is not the ticket that it once was to achieve career advancement. Nowadays, in fact, a degree is nothing more than an entry ticket into the prospect of having a career. The differentiation workers require gets built through the acquisition of practical real-life experience in the career trenches. No amount of education can accelerate or minimize that need for practical experience.

Not only are these career adages antiquated, they are creating a career underclass that will find it harder to advance in today's hypercompetitive and rapidly evolving business environment. Career professionals need to continue to be flexible, agile, and adaptable to survive and thrive. It's also essential that they co-opt the same techniques that have enabled manufacturing and information technology to survive, including:

a) **Continuous Learning:** Too many people believe that learning stops once they have completed their formal education, whether college or university. This is far from the truth. We are all learning on a daily basis, whether it's something as commonplace as meeting a new individual or grappling with a new process instigated by a change at work. It's important to recognize that learning both formally and informally is a lifelong and continuous process to ensure the right behaviors are adopted.

b) **Diversified Learning:** While the need to be a subject matter expert in a small number of fields or subjects remains constant, it's also essential to learn about different subjects that may not be adjacent to our everyday tasks. In today's complex and rapidly changing business environment, what's considered leading edge today can be obsolete tomorrow.

If Silicon Valley has taught us anything, it is the fact that innovation and creativity can come from a multitude of unexpected avenues. Innovation and creativity is driven when individuals take disparate ideas and create something unique. Such melding is a messy and non-linear process but it has created some of the greatest advancements of our time. From social media to ride sharing, new business models have been created because individuals were willing to step outside of their educational "ivory towers" and see how other schools of thought can be leveraged and applied.

c) **Moving Beyond One's Comfort Zone on Both Personal and Professional Levels:** Education isn't just about professional certifications. It's about personal development as well. The traditional perception of learning has been too heavily focused on certifications, leaving individuals to contend with the infamous accreditation creep that has pervaded all levels of education. To maintain agility and flexibility in today's business environment, personal development is critical. This can take many forms, from career-oriented personal development—such as improving one's public speaking skills—to more personal forms of development such as overcoming one's fear of heights or trying new foods or experiences completely outside of one's comfort zone.

d) **Failing to See Alternative Perspectives:** In this increasingly customized, personalized, and individualized environment, it can be easy to fall into "groupthink" scenarios. Too many of us only watch, read, and listen to viewpoints and perspectives that conform to our individual biases and perspectives. Unfortunately, such "conformity" is extremely dangerous, not only from a societal perspective but an individual one as well. It prevents career-oriented individuals from seeing the reality of their situation and creates roadblocks to making the adjustments that are required to continue surviving and thriving.

In today's complex business environment, no career professional is safe. While the focus has been on the challenges blue-collar workers face, white-collar workers will increasingly struggle with the same issues as automation and artificial intelligence continue to improve and develop. Thus, for any career professional to continue to find long-term satisfaction, you must remember three words: "Always Be Adapting."

10 TREAT YOURSELF LIKE A CORPORATION

As prior economic downturns have taught us, the nature of employment is changing. Jobs that involve routine are rapidly disappearing and being devalued through technology. Traditional nine-to-five jobs are increasingly scarce relative to the available global labor force. Career paths that were once the norm for Baby Boomers no longer exist.

Increasingly, lower-level positions are turning into employment ghettos. Interns are finding themselves moving from one internship to the next, never able to find an entry level-position due to outsourcing and downsizing. Mid-level positions have vanished thanks to increasing devolution of responsibilities to junior levels.

With all the changes occurring, one wonders how anyone can succeed in this work environment. The simple answer is to emulate those who have profited and thrived, and no group has thrived more than corporations.

Even in these turbulent and unpredictable times, corporations are reaping substantial profits. Treating yourself like a corporation may seem impossible, since a corporation has thousands of individual workers. However, the reality is that we already see numerous examples of individuals treating themselves as corporations. From celebrities to consultants and even entrepreneurs, today's successful individuals rely heavily on corporate characteristics to succeed.

What does it take for individuals to treat themselves like a corporation? There are three foundational elements and six core principles that should be applied. The three foundational elements are:

1) **Experience:** It's not only about longevity—accumulating true battle experience also enables survival in today's economic environment. Corporations and individuals that have survived in difficult times and thrived in goods ones build war chests of knowledge and flexibility that are invaluable for effectively responding to an unknown future.

2) **Networks:** The network multiplier effect is critical for both corporations and individuals. Networks expand and multiply the reach and capabilities of both individuals and corporations, and are crucial for future growth opportunities.

3) **Capabilities:** The core of any successful corporation is the capability to tackle future challenges. For individuals, this involves gaining the right skills and education for career advancement.

Having established the three foundational elements, a number of principles are essential for individuals to successfully treat themselves like a corporation. Just like a corporation, individuals need a series of core strategic principles to guide their career moves:

a) **Define Clear Goals and Objectives:** A common excuse for not having clear goals and objectives is lacking necessary information to make informed decisions. And truthfully, we very rarely have enough data points to make a truly informed decision. However, most individuals have amassed enough life experience to provide a good gauge of their own satisfaction, thus providing an opportunity to set appropriate career goals and objectives.

b) **Determine What Capabilities You Possess and How They Compare to the Market:** People are proud of themselves when they complete a university degree or a difficult certification. However, while individual achievements need to be celebrated, one must always be aware that capabilities constantly need to be upgraded. A unique capability in 2007 might not be relevant in 2017.

c) **Determine If You Have a Unique Value Proposition or Are a Commodity:** It's essential to take an honest look at your personal value proposition to determine your uniqueness. Do you offer something fundamentally unique or are you an easily replaceable widget? Unique individuals can protect themselves better in today's economy and can demand more for their services in return.

d) **Treat Every Job As a Building Block:** The reality of today's business environment is a job is no longer "just a job," but rather a building block to achieve one's goals and objectives. Jobs are not just for funding daily subsistence, but rather about building an individual's foundational elements. No matter how mundane, a job must offer some value besides a monetary one that can be translated into career advancement.

e) **Start Internally and Externally Differentiating:** Differentiation is not achieved overnight. It's done in incremental steps and relies heavily on building all three corporate elements (experience, networks, capability) to achieve both internal and external differentiation. While internal differentiation is the easier of the two to achieve (e.g., being the top sales performer), one should never forget about the external differentiation. Ensuring the wider market is aware of one's "uniqueness" creates future growth opportunities.

f) **Always Be Looking:** With the accepted expectation that today's individuals will have multiple jobs during their careers, it's increasingly critical to proactively look for future opportunities. Whether through conferences or trade events, individuals need to be looking for the next better and bigger position to achieve their goals and objectives.

These six principles combined with the three foundational elements will provide you with a solid framework on which to build your careers. This framework is flexible enough to be leveraged by individuals climbing the traditional corporate ladder or taking alternative career paths.

Today's economy is a volatile one for individuals. Nothing is a foregone conclusion and nothing is permanent. Corporations are the best example of an entity that has managed to survive a dynamic and ever-changing environment. While not a perfect metaphor, it's one that is increasingly relevant in today's dynamic business landscape.

11 WHAT THEY DON'T TEACH YOU ABOUT LEADERSHIP IN MBA SCHOOL

The most common mistake that MBA graduates make is the belief that they are now true leaders. The reality is far from the truth. The most that MBA graduates have achieved is the acquisition of business knowledge that's already been rendered stale by the rapid pace of change.

Leading individuals and organizations is not taught in MBA school, but rather learned from the experiences gained on the business battlefield. Indeed, leadership is less about acquiring more knowledge and more about developing the skills required to lead the most valuable, stubbornly problematic resource available: human beings.

Leadership isn't imbued through a formal process or through a formal title. It's thrust upon people in the most subtle and informal ways. Those ready to accept the leadership mantle are incredibly self-aware and also perceptive about those around them.

That self-awareness is critical as one takes on a leadership role. Indeed, it's crucial in making the transition from a mere individual contributor to a leader. Without self-awareness, leaders will never be able to create the conditions for achieving exceptional results from their teams and themselves.

I have learned there are several key principles to strong leadership

1) **Words Matter, but So Does Their Delivery:** People remember what is spoken to them. They might not necessarily remember it verbatim, but they will remember the general context and intent. It's not surprising that many people forget this, particularly if they've been overly focused on "book smarts" versus "street smarts."

Inexperienced leaders may tend to think of words as just words. Savvy leaders, on the other hand, know that the delivery of a message is critical to ensuring that it resonates in the appropriate manner.

2) **Both Subtle and Direct Actions Count:** Actions matter in management. Without tackling direct action, leaders (a) aren't credible to their teams and to their organization, and (b) aren't fulfilling their mandates as leaders to produce quantifiable and tangible results.

But subtle actions are just as important. They're less about concrete results and more about the team motivation and organization required to achieve those results. Strong leaders must find the optimal methods to motivate individual team members.

While every leader has their own unique leadership style, their ability to execute on subtle actions is critical to develop the environment for superior performance. What do I mean by subtle actions?

When it comes to leadership, interpersonal skills are critical. That includes listening to both verbal and nonverbal cues, and also the actions that are generated from that listening. This is where subtle actions come in.

It's about taking actions that haven't necessarily been requested but are appreciated nonetheless. An example of one such action might be celebrating an employee's personal (i.e., non-work-related) accomplishment such as finishing a personal film project. In other words, it isn't about listening to your team purely for work purposes—you also need to leverage the cues that will help build personal relationships.

3) **True Leadership Is Earned:** There is a belief that leadership just happens. The reality is that leadership isn't thrust upon individuals suddenly, but rather is a gradual process that often happens behind the scenes.

That said, leadership is sometimes awarded through political maneuvering, pre-existing privilege, or even just plain old luck, but earned leadership is gained via small discrete actions. Too many people believe that leadership can be earned through a mere designation, but the reality is that leadership is incrementally demonstrated via experience and gained on the battlefield of real life and not in classroom simulations.

4) **Results Still Matter, But Now You Have to Rely on Others:** The expression popularized by President Harry Truman, "the buck stops here," still rings true. Today's leaders must be able to execute basic tasks flawlessly, but that also means they need to rely on the efforts of others more than ever.

Leadership requires leveraging the available resources around you in the most optimal manner possible. Increasingly, what differentiates great leaders from good leaders is their ability to instill a sense of both individual empowerment and common vision amongst the people and organizations they lead. Today's effective leaders know that it's not about how many widgets a team member can produce and more about how their leadership can spark the next multibillion dollar idea.

5) **Preparation Is Critical:** Leaders don't breezily walk into a situation and believe that they can instantaneously produce the correct answer. That's Hollywood fantasy.

The reality is that leaders do an inordinate amount of preparation prior to any meeting. And that's not just about giving the appearance that they actually know what they're talking about—it ensures that the meeting ends in a direction that works for their short- and long-term interests. Leaders set the tone in terms of how the meeting is conducted and also make sure that the meeting is productive, with clear actionable goals. Indeed, some would say post-meeting actions are more critical than the meeting itself and that leaders who don't understand this are merely using the meeting for self-aggrandizement.

12 HOW NOT TO MANAGE PEOPLE

Due to the growth of organizations on an international scale, the demand for management personnel has never been greater. Whether it is leading a multinational project or a large internal team, organizations are pressing individuals into management roles at a greater pace than ever before.

While demand continues to grow, supply is still limited due to a number of factors, including:

1) **Flattened Hierarchical Structures:** Globally, organizations are becoming increasingly flat and lack the middle management layer that once existed. While eliminating middle management has improved the bottom line, it has also removed an invaluable resource and training ground for future managers. Future managers no longer have the mentorship and guidance from middle management required to learn from past errors.

2) **Immediate Need:** Unfortunately, the speed with which the global economy moves and the increasing need for agility within organizations force many individuals into management duties merely as a result of them being the most qualified on the team. There is no longer a gradual ramp up to a management position. Rather, it is one where an individual is thrown into the deep end and told to "sink or swim."

3) **Lack of Training Programs:** As cost pressures continue to mount in today's hypercompetitive economy, organizations are cutting back

on in-house training. This means that individuals placed in management roles are left to their own devices in terms of acquiring the right management skills.

Not only does bad management destroy employee morale and decreases productivity, in today's social media–saturated world, it can result in negative brand connotations, thus hurting future employee prospects.

The following list is illustrative of some of the bone-headed behaviors of managers who fail to understand that their role is not just to push paper but rather to be a visionary leader who motivates people while improving processes. It is by no means exhaustive:

a) **Lacking Cultural Sensitivity:** Today's managers have to manage appropriately for the 21st and not the 19th century. This means dealing with a diverse, multicultural workforce with varying needs and requirements. Today's diversity parameters are much more than just the standard ones of gender, race, religion, or sexual orientation, but also include individual diversity. Whether it is a single mother taking care of two children or a son taking care of an ailing father with Alzheimer's disease, today's managers must deal with individuals as people with real, complicated lives and not merely widgets.

b) **Feeding Your Employees to the Wolves:** One of the biggest failures of new managers is their inability to understand that they are not only responsible for their own personal career but also for the individual members of their team. For a manager, this means that they need to protect their team from unreasonable demands of both senior management and clients. A skilled manager provides his or her team with the support and backup needed to ensure that there are no unreasonable demands made on them. Leaving individual team members to fend for themselves in the face of unreasonable requests makes one question the value of a manager and also negatively impacts the team.

c) **Being Reactive:** One of the biggest challenges for new managers is overcoming the ingrained reactive persona that's all too common in the workplace and becoming a proactive manager instead. However, proactivity no longer means merely being able to foresee and circumvent roadblocks to the successful conclusion of a project. In today's hypercompetitive business environment, it also entails envisioning where the team will need to be in three months, six months and 12 months as the business environment changes and forces a shift in strategy.

d) **Not Effectively Listening:** In the cacophony of today's hypercompetitive business environment, it's too easy for messages and communications to get lost in the fray. All too often, new managers who, during their initial employment, were individual contributors and had to fight for recognition, continue to adopt the aggressive active persona. We have all seen this before. An individual who takes a "my way or the highway" approach to managing people that demotivates them rather than motivates them. What a team really needs from new managers is a change in persona from the aggressive active one to a persona that is based on truly listening to the team. One that emphasizes actively listening to their concerns and actively relaying information that truly addresses those concerns rather than with standard pabulum.

e) **Lack of Forward Momentum:** Today's business environment changes so rapidly that success is no longer merely about pushing paper, but also about progress for both the organization and the individual employee. Forward momentum is required for everything that an organization and its teams do. If a manager can't provide this momentum, team morale suffers, and the team's very reason for existence gets questioned as well.

f) **Not Communicating:** Communication should be the primary goal of managers, whether it's team processes and metrics, or transparency about their own daily schedules. A failure to communicate relevant and factual information to the team not only reduces morale, but productivity as well. Furthermore, it has the potential to increase dissension within the team as well.

With so many active organizations—tackling increasingly complex projects with a diverse staff—good managers are more critical than ever. Knowing some of the behaviors to avoid will make managers more successful, and also improve overall team productivity and morale.

13 WHAT ARE YOU LEARNING FOR?

As the economy continues its transition to a more knowledge-based marketplace, it's more important than ever to make smart education choices. Obviously education can present huge financial (and non-financial) costs, but it also determines how difficult it is to transition from one chosen field to another. That being said, however, an individual can't base their educational path on career alone.

Education is an increasingly politicized topic of contention. Politicians continue to hammer away at the fact that national competitive advantage is being eroded because there aren't enough individuals who are trained in science, technology, engineering, and mathematics. But that's the wrong area to focus on, both from an individual and societal perspective.

In an age of automation and machine learning, it's critical for everyone—whether they are an employee or an employer—to adopt a life-long learning approach that's tailored to their personal preferences rather than work needs. The reality is that work is increasingly unstable. No one is guaranteed a lifetime role whether they are a CEO, a banker, or even a engineer.

Business models, technology, and the general workplace environment are moving so quickly that no one can stand still. When it comes to education, there needs to be a balanced approach if the economy wants healthy, productive, and creative workers.

The emphasis on education for the sake of work isn't only

shortsighted—it also creates a perpetual cycle of debt. With educational debt increasing to dramatic levels, workers will be become more risk averse and look for stability, both behaviors which are no longer desired in today's economy.

14 EDUCATION FOR CAREER OR EDUCATION FOR LIFE?

As the dynamic global economy continues to hammer away at employee stability, those just starting their postsecondary studies are the most affected. Many students are looking for advice about what degrees to pursue to ensure they extract the most value from their education.

The standard answer that students keep hearing from business leaders is to pursue degrees that are in the greatest demand, such as engineering. From a purely economic perspective, this is logical. However, from a life-knowledge perspective, it's more questionable. Indeed, it begs the question: when did a degree turn into a career stepping stone?

Over the years, there has been a considerable change in the perceived value of a degree as well as its purpose. For Baby Boomers, the "Ivory Tower" persona associated with a postsecondary degree remained intact. The majority of the population could find a middle-class job with only a high school diploma, therefore making the need for a university degree limited. However, the changing nature of the economy has dramatically shifted the value of education.

These days, a high school diploma is no longer sufficient as an entry point into the economy. Today's equivalent of a high school diploma is the undergraduate degree. The transformation of the undergraduate degree as the minimum requirement to enter today's workforce introduces a number of questions, including:

a) Is a postsecondary education meant to be an entry ticket into a career or is it meant to be an exploration of self?
b) Is a postsecondary education meant to merely provide concrete employable skills or abstract reasoning ability?

Postsecondary students are increasingly caught in an eternal struggle regarding the fundamental purpose of education. Business leaders are driving students toward "practical" degrees such as engineering, while other advisers advocate for a comprehensive educational approach that provides students critical analytical abilities.

It's easy to see how the business approach to education is seductive, particularly to students who need secure jobs to pay the student debt they have incurred once they graduate. Business leaders constantly complain about the need for more engineering graduates and claim that they have thousands of positions waiting to be filled. But is this need justified from an individual or even a societal perspective?

The first question that must be asked is if society's best interests are truly served by funneling students into careers that are (a) based on short-term economic needs and (b) focused on technical skills. The one constant that the global economy has demonstrated is that it is unpredictable. What's considered a "hot" career for one generation can disappear with the next. This unpredictability suddenly makes corporations' demand for technically skilled individuals a lot less desirable.

Another question is whether corporations are truly looking out for the long-term interests of employees when they plead for more students to enter "hot" careers, or are they really just looking to society to help reduce costs? With the available labor pool expanding due to the interconnected economy, one must wonder if organizations are merely attempting to ensure that today's highly paid "hot" careers are tomorrow's low income work ghettos.

As a result of the rapid pace of technological change, technical skills need to be constantly upgraded. For example, current tech workers are having to adapt to new cloud-based architecture. The question then becomes: Are employees being forced into continuous lifelong learning and heavier student debt loads for perpetuity?

While the self-interest of organizations and the rapid obsolescence of technical skills are good enough reasons to be wary of leveraging postsecondary institutions as an initial career stepping stone, others strike to the heart of what it truly means to work. It brings up the fundamental question: are we living to work or working to live?

It's accurate that many organizations could have their employee shortages solved overnight if more students entered high-demand fields, but the question is whether or not they should. As many productivity surveys show, the best employees are those who are passionate about their careers. Funneling individuals into fields solely on quantitative metrics such as value does not produce passionate high-performers but rather lifeless drones.

High-performing organizations have proven that culture matters and culture is easily killed when you introduce sub-par performers. Funneling workers into fields based solely on economic value rather than personal preference is not only damaging to the individual but also to the economy and to the society as a whole. Not only could we potentially be losing the next great Picasso, but overall economic and societal productivity could be negatively impacted as well.

The biggest assumption that's made when corralling students into high-demand fields is that that they're fully aware of what they want. The reality is that most young students have absolutely no clue what they want from life or a career. They're exploring who they truly are, particularly since the majority of them are away from parental control for the first time in their lives. This self-exploration is what will truly define what their postsecondary experience should be.

There's no doubt that the need for technically skilled workers has been never greater. However, society must never forget that education is not meant to merely provide meaningful employment: it also provides the analytical foundation to enable individuals to adapt and grow. Humans aren't merely cogs in the machine for vast corporate behemoths but rather ever-changing   individuals   with   free   will.

15 WHAT IS THE NEW WAY OF APPRENTICING?

While there's been much talk about the elimination of middle-class positions in the global economy, the elimination of entry level positions has been woefully under-discussed. The elimination of middle-class positions is only the preliminary wave of the coming tsunami that will dramatically reshape the global economy for generations to come.

Why is this an issue that needs to be addressed now? Because the changes that need to be implemented are systemic in nature and will take years to execute and filter down. In the meantime, it will mean hardship for many people.

There can be no doubt that the decimation of the middle class by automation and machine learning is happening with increasing frequency on a global scale. But what exactly is the impact on the next generation of workers? Specifically, some ways in which it might affect entry-level positions include:

1) **Eliminating Positions:** In all sectors of employments, from blue collar to white collar. entry-level positions are being eliminated. In the past, individuals could conceivably climb the corporate ladder from the mailroom clerk to CEO, but these days entry-level positions such as the mailroom clerk have been automated out of existence, whether through technology or changing business behaviors.

2) **Eliminating an Avenue to Develop Basic Career Skills:** Talk to any successful entrepreneur or businessperson today and they will

look back upon their first job as the training ground for the behaviors that powered them to greatness. Unfortunately, today's entry-level positions don't look like the ones of the past. Basic job skills such as punctuality, proper office behavior, etc. can be tough to learn without these positions. Postsecondary institutions would state from their ivory tower positions that their responsibility is to ensure graduates have the mental agility to climb the corporate ladder, and that providing "basic" career skills isn't their responsibility. But that begs the question: whose responsibility is it then?

3) **Eliminating a Rung on the Corporate Ladder:** Thanks to automation and machine learning, the corporate ladder has had a rung removed from the corporate ladder. Unfortunately, that bottom rung was critical to many an individual in terms of not only acquiring the right skills to climb the corporate ladder but as a means of sustenance while waiting for the opportunity to climb. Indeed, the lowly corporate rung not only provided a means of economic survival but the ability for individuals to build a network and gain experience critical to climbing the corporate ladder.

If we've eliminated the starting rung on the corporate ladder, what will replace it? It's a critical question that has yet to be answered. Indeed, current and future generations must address it as we potentially face increasing levels of unemployment due to a reduction of positions. Unfortunately, the answers aren't easy to come by and are highly complex. Potential solutions include:

a) **Clearly Define What Basic Career Skills Are:** Both society and businesses have in some respect failed to clearly define what basic career skills are. Instead, we've left it up to ambiguous social cues and training to provide those skills. And the reality is only those who are truly self-aware understand what they are being taught and why it will benefit them over the long term. We need to change this in order to grow the required future employee base.

b) **Determine Who Is Responsible for Providing Basic Career Skills:** Employers, governments, and educational institutions must all make efforts to enable individuals to easily acquire the basic career skills needed to thrive and climb the corporate ladder. Forcing individuals to haphazardly determine the appropriate course of action for them not only wastes their precious time and resources, it also reduces the pool of desperately needed talent to grow the economy.

c) **Develop a Path to Gain Basic Career Skills:** While the ultimate responsibility of learning basic career skills is up to the individual, providing an easy to navigate path is the responsibility of all parties involved particularly if we want a productive employee base. Not only will providing such a path relieve the stress of decision-making on the part of individuals but it will also ensure that the next generation of employees are trained as well or better than the previous generation.

In our increasingly competitive global economy where jobs are quickly changing—if not being outright eliminated due to technology and automation—we need to ensure that individuals have a clear path to basic career skills. Without it, we are dooming a significant part of society to perpetual poverty and hindering the overall growth of the economy.

16 WHAT IS THE REAL PURPOSE OF A RESUME?

One of the biggest issues with resumes is a misunderstanding about what they're supposed represent: the uniqueness of a prospective employee.

For too long, resumes have been treated as a necessary evil one needs to create when looking for a new opportunity. The sad throwaway nature of resumes belittles a candidate's accomplishments. A well-crafted resume, on the other hand, tells organizations what a candidate has accomplished, what they can potentially do, and whether their personal values fit with the organization's. Ultimately, a resume is a dynamic timeline of an individual's personal and professional accomplishments, values, and future dreams. Unfortunately, we too often don't treat it as such.

Many individuals only look at their resume when they are forced to look for a new job. But for resumes to be effective, they must be treated as a living document, one that constantly grows and needs pruning. This is particularly important in today's dynamic economy. The "jobs for life" mentality of the past made it easy to forget about one's resume after landing your first job. Why update one's resume if you expected to stay with one organization? That mentality, though, was just as misguided then as it is now.

Even if an individual manages to be a "career lifer" at one organization, the reality is that their role will change not only due to personal ambition but through naturally gained experience and, of course, time. A resume, even for a career lifer, is a critical memory document of what accomplishments an individual achieved over the course of their career.

Without a continuously updated resume, individuals miss out not only on advancement opportunities but accomplishments and achievements that could provide insight on the next step of their career journey.

As much as we'd like to think that our memories are flawless, the reality is far different. Our recollections are highly selective, and comprise only one perspective on a situation. To overcome these flaws, individuals must take the effort to record their individual career accomplishments in a timely manner, even if it just means keeping a list of achievements. In addition, the record should be as detailed as possible. It should include what you actually did and how it positively impacted the organization. Why is this critical?

Having an unvarnished record of one's career accomplishments and achievements provides insight into one's past and also clues about what they want to achieve in the future. These individual personal insights are critical to charting a path of fulfillment and happiness in today's dynamic economy.

By having a detailed record of one's career accomplishments and achievements unfiltered by time and personal bias, your resume will be more impactful, and also contain sufficient detail to drive home your impact on an organization and express your career desires.

By using the detailed record and reviewing it over time, you'll begin to detect patterns that can give insight into your career preferences and areas of development. Indeed, many people don't realize that as they progress in their careers, they develop noticeable patterns, and those patterns can be seen in their detailed record.

Patterns aren't necessarily a bad thing, particularly when it comes to determining what someone is passionate about. It's also a good way to measure reality against aspirations. It enables you to be reflective about your accomplishments. In other words, it allows you to truly figure out your passion away from the heat of the moment.

It can also be used to determine areas where you need to improve or gain experience to achieve your career goals. For instance, if an individual is interested in pursuing a career in management consulting, a detailed record may reveal that their quantitative skills are lacking and that their next position should be more quantitative-based.

In the end, a detailed analysis provides a good roadmap for skills an individual needs for career advancement, and also offers and emotional booster for those who think their career is stalled. Reviewing your career path reminds you of your achievements and gives you that extra boost of energy to continue to pursue your career goals.

17 WHAT REALLY NEEDS TO BE ON YOUR RESUME

While there is a common belief that resumes are relatively standard, truthfully that standard lies in the eye of the beholder. An "effective" resume for an investment banker would be totally inappropriate for a user experience designer. One needs to tailor their resume to not only meet the expectations of the industry but enables them to truly shine a light on their accomplishments in a personalized fashion. Resumes are your first and perhaps only tool to market yourself to a potential employer. As such, you must treat it with the respect it deserves. What does this mean tactically?

There are a number of elements that need to be taken into account when crafting a resume:

1) **Tell a Story:** Everyone loves a story. Stories are memorable, much more so than a list of facts and figures. It's critical that your resume be memorable so that whoever's reading it will keep you in mind as they filter through a stack of them.

   Developing a memorable story enables a resume writer to determine what they want from a position, and what they want from a career as well. Good stories have a beginning, a middle, and an end. Many individuals don't craft their resumes with that in mind and it shows. Some merely use them as a data dump of work history, boring readers and severely reducing their chances of landing an interview.

   Thinking about storytelling forces individuals to figure out what story they want to tell about their career—past, present, and future. But it can be hard to keep this mind when you're mostly focused on income to sustain yourself and your loved ones. However, even in such circumstances, it is possible to tell a story.

There are usually commonalities across positions in an individual's work history that will allow them to tell a basic story if not a detailed one. By determining a basic story, you're planting the initial seeds for building a career that you'll be happy with.

2) **Start with Experience First:** Obviously education and credentials are important for career advancement, but it's ultimately experience that differentiates employees. Unfortunately, though, too many resume writers continue to follow the old format from their college days, highlighting their education first instead of their experience.

It isn't illogical for college students to highlight their education as it's the only differentiator they have on a relatively thin resume. It is true that many will have summer positions, but those positions are more to learn the basics of the workplace than a true career. For many, their college degree is the first true indicator of what career they are interested in and that's why they place their education first on their resume.

The reality is that the experience one builds in the workforce is actually more relevant as one grows in their career.

3) **Demonstrate Value Add:** Too many resume writers list every little task they accomplished at work. Not only does that bury their resume in meaningless minutia; it also prevents you from actually telling a clear and attention-grabbing story.

To be clear, the value add you want to convey is for the employer. Focus on the tasks and activities that directly contributed to adding value to an employer. And while it might be tempting to focus on the financial impact of these task, keep in mind that in today's economy social impact is increasingly valued.

It may seem difficult to quantify the value you've added to an employer if you were several steps removed from the actual levers that create value. But don't sell yourself short. The reality is that every position within an employer drives value even though that individual might be two or three steps away from pulling the actual value-creation lever. Demonstrating that you understanding this on your resume is a good way to enhance your storytelling.

18 RESUME BLUNDERS

There are some common errors in resumes that can damage a candidate's prospects at getting an initial interview.

These errors reflect a poor ability to tell a coherent story about the applicant. Career counsellors fail to impart that basic knowledge to resume writers, thus forcing recruiters to wade through bad resumes. Some of these common failures include:

1) **Turning a Resume Into a Data Dump:** Too many resumes look like a data dump of every single task an individual has accomplished. This wastes the time and effort of the recruiter as it prevents them from effectively identifying high-potential candidates.

   It's far better to highlight specific tasks that (a) added value to the organization in terms of operational and financial gain and (b) demonstrate individual leadership and foresight.

2) **Using MBA Speak:** With limited real estate on a resume, there is a great tendency for individuals to turn to "MBA speak." Everyone has seen this MBA speak. It's using impressive-sounding words that don't represent everyday language and have very little actual meaning.

   MBA speak isn't just meaningless: it harms the chances of an individual advancing. Not only does will it fail to differentiate the candidate, it will also plant seeds of doubt about whether the individual actually did the work.

Resume writers should not be afraid to use common language to describe value-added tasks in detail. Indeed, common language demonstrates that the individual might have actually done the work and is also easily understood by a recruiter.

3) **Not Giving Enough Detail:** Too many resumes provide task descriptions at such a high level as to be meaningless. Most individuals believe that providing one compact description of what they have done will demonstrate their brilliance, but that's far from the truth. While such descriptions are critical to peaking a recruiter's interest, the reality is that more detail is required to truly convince a recruiter of their accomplishments.

Providing additional details about what obstacles had to be overcome not only convinces the recruiter that an individual actually accomplished the task but also demonstrates value-add potential.

4) **Not Telling the Organization What Value You Can Bring to a Specific Position:** While a significant number of organizations are acknowledging that cultural fit is an increasingly critical component, it's important to remember that's a secondary concern in the hiring process. It's great if you believe in the vision, but if you can't fulfill the position role and responsibilities, you won't get hired.

While these are only a few of the resume blunders that many recruiters see, they are some of the most grievous. These errors are likely to prevent individuals from getting an initial interview, and consign your resume to the dustbin of mediocrity.

19 THE DOS AND DON'TS OF NETWORKING

In our complex economy, the need to network has never been greater. Networking is the lifeblood of business. Unfortunately, there's not enough education about networking skills, so most people must blindly navigate through the process.

There's a common belief that networking is a natural born ability that they either people have or they don't. The reality though is that networking is like any other skill—it can be learned no matter how naturally disinclined someone is to it. A failure to learn networking stems more from an unwillingness to learn than anything else. Like many things in one's career, networking is about finding what is comfortable for the individual and developing a system to make it happen.

Networking is an elusive activity with its own rituals that can't be learned from a textbook. Most experienced networkers hone their abilities through a combination of self-awareness and self-adjustment as well as continual practice and refinement.

While networking is very much a personalized activity that needs to be individually customized, there are some general guidelines that can be provided. Networking is much more an art than a science, but having some guidelines not only ensures the development of good behaviors, it also ensures greater efficacy.

The following list of dos and don'ts isn't comprehensive and is merely meant as a set of guidelines:

The Dos of Networking

1) **Long Term Planning and Execution:** Most consummate networkers know that to be successful at networking it's important to focus on the long term versus the short term. Whether you're working on building your career or developing a strategic sales partnership, actions have long-lasting repercussions as previous actions build on current and future ones. Networking is very similar.

With today's globalized economy, you never know where your career will take you. The same goes for your network. Individuals are increasingly changing positions on a frequent basis. As such, the consummate networker knows that while a network connection might not be of value at present, it may be critical in the future.

2) **Understand and Articulate Your Value:** One of the biggest challenges inexperienced networkers face is understanding and articulating their own value. As career paths get less stable and predictable in today's economy, most networkers can't rely solely on their current role as defining their networking value. Today's networker has to think holistically concerning the value they not only offer now but what they will offer in the future as well.

Failing to articulate your value beyond your current position sets you up for short-term sales pitches more often than not. Experienced networkers know how to not only succinctly sum up their value proposition in a single phrase (e.g., "experienced super-connector"), but also know how to weave a memorable story that concretely demonstrates their value proposition over the long term.

3) **Follow Up Promptly:** Most networking pros know that human memory is a fleeting thing. If you don't promptly follow up with a new connection, that person will forget and move onto the next networker. While it's true that technology (e.g., LinkedIn and similar CRM tools) has improved our memories when it comes to building connections, nothing builds a longer lasting networking relationship than reinforcing the positive feeling made during the initial point of contact.

What defines prompt? Following up within 24 hours is probably the most impactful. Within 48 hours is also acceptable but anything afterwards will have exponentially lower positive outcomes.

4) **Pay It Forward:** Networking isn't only about you and your career goals. It's about building a strong network of individuals that grows on each other's successes. Networking success comes in all forms. Whether it's providing a referral or the right introductions to fund a start-up, "paying it forward" within the network will pay dividends as the network's successes multiply and bear fruit. Indeed, fostering a "pay it forward" network will be ultimately be more rewarding than one that's purely dominated by self-interest.

The Don'ts of Networking

1) **Don't Be a "Wayward Networker":** Networking isn't a one-off game. The most common mistake that individuals make is to only network when they need to. These "wayward networkers" are the most aggravating type of networkers due to the fact that they don't realize (a) networking is about building long-term value and (b) about being top of mind while providing value.

   Every consummate networker knows the "wayward networker." They have most aspects of their pitch down (e.g., value proposition, execution, etc.), and they take the first critical steps to build the initial connections. Where they fail, however, is once they have built the first tenuous link, they disappear until they need something again.

   What these "wayward networkers" fail to realize is that their behaviour is not only is the antithesis to the principles of networking, it also hardens the receptiveness and openness of networkers for others. By pulling the networking equivalent of a "dine and dash," a networker becomes more cynical and less willing to help others, thus increasing the barriers that future networkers must overcome to develop the proper networking relationships.

2) **Don't Try to Sell a Product or Service:** The consummate networker knows that selling a product or service while networking is the worst possible approach. Selling a product or service while networking has the feeling of being an unwilling participant in a holiday timeshare presentation. Selling a product or service while networking turns most people off and makes people believe that they are the equivalent of spam for their network.

3) **Don't Communicate for the Sake of Communicating. Make Sure There Is Value:** Valuable communications are those that add value to an individual's personal or professional lives. This communications could be anywhere from forwarding a link for a relevant event to making introductions to individuals who are relevant personal or professional connections. It does not mean sending generic holiday greetings that clog a networker's inbox needlessly.

The preceding guidelines were not meant to be exhaustive but to help prevent networkers from making some basic mistakes that prevent them from successfully making valuable connections.

Happy networking!

20 MAKE YOUR CAREER YOUR OWN

After reading this e-book, I hope that you feel better equipped with the tools necessary to advance your career. But career progression is not just about tools—it's also about your mindset. As I've emphasized throughout this e-book, there is no one truth path for anyone in today's dynamic and rapidly moving global economy. The reality is that we are in the midst of a transition from being mere widgets in the economic system to an age where it is critical that individuals find their true passion.

In many respects, this transition period, while difficult, is a chance for individuals and society to truly understand the value of work from a personal and a societal context. As automation is increasingly used to handle repetitive tasks, what's needed now are individuals with passion and creativity to drive forward new innovations.

What does this mean for individuals? It requires a new level of self-awareness about their preferences, as well as a new form of self-reliance and independence. This sense of self-reliance and independence puts individuals in full control of their career path and their overall sense of career fulfillment.

Thanks to the very technologies and business models that are creating these dynamic conditions, individuals are more empowered than ever to take control of their careers. Whether it is learning a new skill or building their professional network, individuals have far greater opportunities today to shape their careers. Unfortunately, many of us are taught and still believe that success is societally driven and not shaped primarily by personal expectations.

I've encountered too many stories about people who have succeeded in their respective professions only to come to the realization that they aren't happy with what they are doing. They have come to the self-realization that success is not what society tells them but what they individually tell themselves. Often, they've come to this conclusion as the result of painful self discovery, but they're usually happier for it in the end.

In many respects, I have written this e-book as a call to to empower yourself when it comes to your career. Yes, life does throw obstacles in our way, but life wouldn't be worth living if we didn't find a way to overcome those obstacles. We must realize that our individual contentment doesn't come from following one linear path, and that it's possible to enjoy the learning experiences we encounter on our individual journeys.

ABOUT THE AUTHOR

Eric Quon-Lee is a seasoned cross-border management consultant currently based in San Francisco, California with several years of management consulting experience primarily in finance, strategy and operations.

Prior to his current role, Eric has worked for several leading Canadian corporations in aerospace, telecommunications and financial services. In his spare time, Eric is highly involved in the startup ecosystem in the San Francisco Bay Area as well as globally as a "super-connector". Eric has a MBA from the Rotman School of Management – University of Toronto.

72399619R00047

Made in the USA
Middletown, DE
05 May 2018